Pulling Down Stronghold

PULLING DOWN STRONGHOLDS KIT

BY MATTHEW TUCKER

REVISED & UPDATED

Pulling Down Strongholds Kit – Matthew Tucker

Copyright © 2020 by Matthew Wayne Tucker

Website: https://bit.ly/m/ekballohub
Email: ekballoministries@gmail.com

First published in Great Britain in 2020 by Ekballo Ministries

ISBN: 9798567960028

All rights reserved. No part of this publication may be reproduced or distributed in any form or by any means, or stored in a database or retrieval system, without the prior written permission of the author.

Unless otherwise indicated, all Scripture quotations marked (KJV) are from the King James Version®.

Public domain 1611 Scripture quotations from The Authorized (King James) Version.
Rights in the Authorized Version in the United Kingdom are vested in the Crown. Reproduced by permission of the Crown's patentee, Cambridge University Press.
Used by permission. All rights reserved.

Word studies conducted using Strongest Strong's Exhaustive Concordance of the Bible, The: 21st Century Edition ® Copyright © 2001 by Zondervan. Used by permission. All rights reserved.

All emphases in scripture quotations are added by the author.

Contents

About the Author — 1

Introduction — 3

Chapter 1 What are strongholds? — 4

Chapter 2 The purpose of strongholds? — 6

Chapter 3 What is a stronghold composed of? — 7

Chapter 4 How long its supply last? — 9

Chapter 5 How are strongholds formed? — 10

Chapter 6 Does a stronghold = possession? — 14

Chapter 7 Where do demons originate from? — 15

Chapter 8 Signs that you have strongholds? — 18

Chapter 9 Altars and trading platforms. — 20

Chapter 10 Exhaustive list – states of mind. — 34

Chapter 11 How-to pull-down strongholds? — 38

Chapter 12 3 dimensions of freedom. — 46

Chapter 13 Framing and Reframing — 50

Chapter 14 Building the Fortress of the Lord — 58

Pulling Down Strongholds Kit – Matthew Tucker

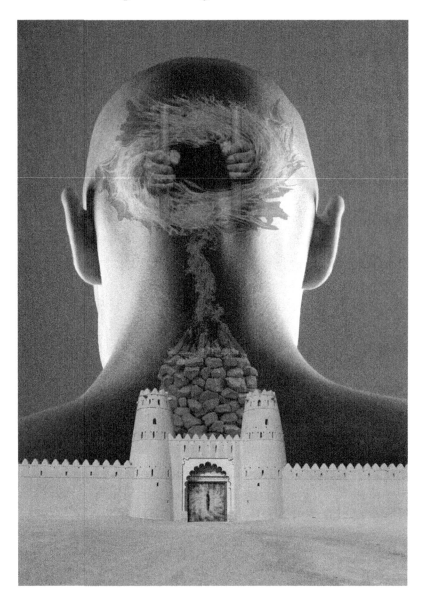

About the Author

Matthew Tucker was born again in November of 2005 and encountered the love and presence of God while hearing the voice of God in the same instance.

He pursued the presence of God and the word of God from that moment on and was baptised in the Holy Spirit in December of 2006 after completing the Mastering Leadership course through Kensington Temple.

It was prophesied that he would understand the mysteries of God, move in healings, miracles, signs, and wonders, and receive an eloquent tongue of the learned to speak the word in season and wisdom which none of his adversaries would be able to contend or speak against.

He is a power evangelist that operates in the prophetic and frequently has heavenly encounters, visions, and dreams.

He is passionate about manifesting the knowledge of the glory of God, unity in the body of Christ, abiding union with God, soul-winning, healing ministry, miracles, spiritual warfare, and deliverance. He also has a keen interest in biology, physics, quantum physics, neuroscience, and pneumatology.

It is his mission to transform the culture of a generation for the expansion and the manifestation of God's Kingdom on the earth.

He was ordained as a Pastor and Evangelist under Eagle Christian Fellowship in 2011. He now lives in Telford England and has been married for over 15 years and has 4 children.

By earthly trade, he has worked in the film and TV industry, youth work, and mainstream education as well as private tutoring since 2010. He is now self-employed and in full-time ministry with his wife, running Ekballo ministries and operating mobile healing rooms and discipleship training, ministering in home churches and on the streets.

Introduction

This book is arguably the most straight forward and to the point guide that you can find and use to pull down strongholds and break soul ties.

This explains what precisely strongholds are, what their purpose is, what they are made of, the origins of demons and how to deal with strongholds and their effects, simply and directly.

This is a small but powerful must have kit that you can use for yourself and to help others get free also.

I wanted to create something that pretty much gets as practical as possible and fast! When there are strongholds causing trouble, you don't want to have to read through hundreds and hundreds of pages to finally get to the last chapter and there you find the practical steps towards deliverance and liberation, for most that takes too long, and with all of the difficulties, temptations, troubles and attacks this current age has to throw at the walk of a believer, it's high time to cut the fluff and just get down to business, so here it is as requested, the pulling down strongholds kit!

PULLING DOWN STRONGHOLDS KIT

***2 Corinthians 10:3** For though we walk in the flesh, we do not war after the flesh: **4** (For the weapons of our warfare [are] not carnal, but mighty through God to the pulling down of strong holds;) **5** Casting down imaginations, and every high thing that exalteth itself against the knowledge of God, and bringing into captivity every thought to the obedience of Christ;*

What are strongholds?

They are structures that are set up in the mind of a person that keeps them in a negative cycle of some kind to create bondages that are very difficult to break, which feed energy into demonic systems and purposes. It provides a place of safety, a fortification of defence for demonic beings and their activity to be connected to someone's life by way of the mind.

2 Corinthians 10:4,5

Luke 11: 21 When a *(a)*<u>strong man</u> *(b)*<u>armed</u> *(c)*<u>keepeth</u> his *(d)*<u>palace</u>, his *(e)*<u>goods</u> are in *(f)*peace:

Luke 11:21: *(a)*Evil Spirit, *(b)*Dark weapons, attacks, negative thoughts and influences, *(c)*Guards and does anything it can to keep influence and gain more influence which includes the use and fortification of **strongholds**, *(d)*Person's body and/or soul influenced by the evil spirit, *(e)*Negative energy harvested as a source of sustenance *(f)*Retained in the control of the evil spirit, feeding it, and giving it strength.

22 But when a *(g)*<u>stronger</u> than he *(h)*<u>shall come upon him</u>, and *(i)*<u>overcome him</u>, he *(j)*<u>taketh</u> from him all his *(k)*<u>**armour** wherein he trusted</u>, and *(l)*<u>divideth his spoils</u>.

Luke 11:22: *(g)*The Holy Spirit and the heavenly hosts, (which include the believer), *(h)*Mount an attack against it using spiritual force, *(i)*Cast the devil out, remove the evil spirit out of the person, *(j)*Regain back the territory that was previously occupied, *(k)*The **strongholds** which were used as defence systems and trusted as places of protection for the evil spirit to continue its works of affliction, *(l)*Energy that was harvested and utilised from the soul, and every influence in the mind is now taken back.

What is the purpose of strongholds?

The purpose of a stronghold in the mind is to first gain entrance to the soul, because the mind overlaps the soul. A stronghold is designed to create a layer of chaos in the realm of the soul that allows demonic beings to interface directly with someone's soul to influence it and control it. The goal would be having influence or control over a person's body. Demons are disembodied spirits and to have any influence upon the earth, they need a body to work through.

Without a stronghold first in place in the mind, no demonic entity can successfully remain attached to a person's soul or body, they can try to send attacks against the body in diverse ways, and even attacks against the mind (fiery darts), but they CANNOT attach themselves to the soul without first a stronghold in place as an adhesive connection layer first.

The stronghold causes that area of the soul to become an ideal climate for the nature of the demonic entity, and this climate is what they use to remain locked into the environment of a person's soul to influence them.

2 Corinthians 10:5

Luke 11:24-25

What exactly is a stronghold composed of?

It is made up of negative energy. Negative energy creates empty spaces of disorder within the soul as negative energy opens these broken places like cracks or gaps within the soul for the demonic being to enter to house their presence. Demonic beings do not have an unlimited power supply as they are disconnected from God's virtue. Demons feed on negative energy to survive. They feed on: sin, anger, trauma, hurt, pain, despair, fear, etc, the bad list goes on including all the works of the flesh listed in the Bible.

This power supply of negative energy is what sustains their presence, around or within a person or place, they cannot survive in dry places as spoken of in the Bible, so they seek where they can be sustained. They exchange negative soulish energy from people and need it to have a life support system to keep them having an access point to the land of the living, which is why they cause harm to people (like leeches survive at the expense of other living things).

If they stop, they simply cannot access the earth realm anymore because they lose the life supply of people's souls and then because they do not have any energy that comes from a living soul, which IS DESIGNED TO INTERFACE WITH A BODY, being bodiless themselves, they would eventually disconnect with the earth entirely as their own life support system is starved. Their energy signal winds down further and further till it matches that of hell (which was designed to destroy sin) and they are pulled down into it as if magnetically.

Matthew 6:23

Luke 11:34

How long can a demonic being's spiritual energy supply last?

Is hard to tell, but there is a system in the demonic and a hierarchy, yet no real allegiance. However, their collective: jealousy, hatred and envy of humanity as well as having a need to afflict them to survive, keeps the demons actively seeking to cause harm. They deceive, steal, kill and destroy and they will even collaborate with other demons if that means a greater chance of not just success but eventually gaining more ability to influence and or control a body. They are never satisfied.

If entrance into a body is gained, the body then houses them and they in a sense have hit the jackpot. A near unlimited supply of energy and a place that has been caused to become acclimatized for them because of the stronghold, and they will never want to leave once they have entered; this is where casting out devils comes in and becomes the only solution. The particular administration of casting out devils will be explored in my book 'Deliverance Apparatus'.

Ephesians 6:12

Matthew 8:16

Matthew 10:8

Matthew 12:28

How are strongholds formed

They are formed by agreements that have been made, they cannot be constructed by the demonic entities alone, this is not possible, they do not have the materials or power to cause such structures to be built. Instead, they send attacks to cause the person to alter their thinking into certain patterns which in turn leads to behaviours, habits, and cycles that loop in on themselves negatively. As soon as a negative loop cycle is established that can automate, then a stronghold has just been formed.

The beginning of a stronghold is not a powerful enough structure to create a stable enough layer that can house a demonic being, unless it is embedded deeply enough into a person's thinking to the point where they are so controlled by it that it begins to become a prevalent force that affects their everyday life constantly, then the chaotic structures of this stronghold are solidified enough. Only then can it be a stable enough layer for a demonic being to be able to interface with a person's soul. With a connection made with the soul this begins the process of demonic influence to work on a deeper level in someone's life, all other stages before a stable layer is made are levels of demonic oppression more so than direct influence.

In a similar way that in the old system God inhabits the praises of His people, thanksgiving opens the way to the presence of God and praise begin the habitation process.

This is because one of the functions of praise is to create a platform for heavenly activity to rest on in the earth and connect through into the physical world.

The higher the praise the stronger the signal heaven can connect with, until the atmosphere is so charged with heaven the signals merge together and become one open channel of flow. This is when the power of God permeates into the earth in enormously powerful ways because heaven impregnates the atmosphere with God's world. In worship, this goes even higher and the person of God Himself starts to cause an atmosphere to adjust not just to heaven's signal but the same signal as the throne room in heaven. In the glory a saturation point is reached where the lines are blurred between heaven and earth completely; so much so that a big gateway is formed and fully established in which heaven and earth is geographically and physically bridged and direct spiritual realities and heavenly realities even God Himself crosses over very tangibly.

As glorious as this is, this is still the old system, because now WE are THE habitation of God, and all these things happen on the inside of us (**Luke 17:21** the kingdom of God is within you).

The demonic operates under the opposite processes of the old system (which is invitation, visitation and finally habitation), because it cannot mimic the new system of the kingdom of God within us that was birthed out of Christ and formed the new creation.

So, the demons inhabit the opposite of praise, contention, complaining, and anger, worry, fear etc (invitation), and this progressively intensifies, building a stronghold (visitation). Then possession (habitation), the reverse of the old system.

Romans 1:21

Ephesians 4:18

Proverbs 18:21

Does a stronghold = possession, and mean a person needs deliverance?

No, it does not. A person with strongholds does not always house demonic entities internally (especially when it comes to believers). People may be often oppressed by them, but the presence of strongholds are not always the presence of demons, but the presence of demons are always the presence of strongholds.

A stronghold can be broken and pulled down and a person can be set free from a cycle of behaviour that could have led to their enslavement and eventual demonic control if allowed to worsen and not contended against by the word of God, prayer and renewing the mind. Strongholds need to be replaced with the fortress of the Lord, which is a network of the engrafted word of God which is able to save the soul. The individual who renews their mind and receives with meekness the engrafted word of God will themselves be in health and prosper as their soul prospers and will progressively be increasing in experiencing their freedom in Christ.

Where do demons originate from?
They are the result of the disembodied spirits of the deceased Nephilim, mostly pre-flood, but some post flood in the times of Joshua and Caleb and later the Davidic wars. Because they were constructed of fallen human genome and fallen angelic spiritual matter (which was calibrated to interface with human genetics), which is an inverted spiritual principle, imploded light, dark spiritual light, anti-spiritual matter even. Then out of the mingling of the two entities was spawned a creature that is neither human, nor angel, yet part of both systems in some way and therefore semi compatible with both humans and angels yet not having living souls of their own.

Natural man is connected to the spiritual world of the second heaven and natural world of the first heaven.

Fallen angels are connected to spiritual world of the second heaven and spiritual world of below the earth sheol/underworld and the abyss/pit.

When the Nephilim were killed in the flood, they did not belong anywhere. They were trapped between the places that bridge the earth, the second heaven and the underworld. Once disembodied they became spiritually nomadic. They could not go onto Abraham's bosom (paradise = pre-Christ place of the spirits of the righteous) because they were not human.

They could not go straight into chains of darkness because they were not entirely fallen angel, they could not go straight to hell because of their partial humanity means they require judgement to be issued upon them first to transition them into the places of punishment permanently, so they were stuck upon the earth with nowhere to go.

When Jesus came and judgement was dealt on Him by way of the cross, and His descent into hades and having taken the keys of death and the grave. Demons NOW MUST GO DOWN TO HELL, so now, unless they leech off living souls, <u>their energy system will not allow them to stay upon the earth</u>.

They cannot be saved, they cannot repent; they have no body, no living souls of their own, not of God's image or likeness, they are doomed.

Genesis 6

Book of Enoch Section 1 Chapter 15 verse 3-11

What are signs that you have strongholds which need dealing with?

- Negative <u>cycles</u> that are perpetual and affect multiple areas of your life.
- Negative <u>ways of thinking</u> that can have you <u>trapped</u> in your head.
- Gripped with intense <u>negative emotion</u> that is seemingly beyond control.
- The body is manifesting heightened negative <u>stress-based responses</u>.
- Specific triggers that set off negative responses or cycles <u>automatically</u>.
- Certain people, places, sensory stimulus, times of year, events triggers a <u>negative set of emotions or memories</u> that keep being brought up.
- <u>Obsessive or compulsive</u> behaviour patterns that become embedded rituals.
- If any <u>unusual attachments</u> to certain <u>objects, foods, substances, drugs</u>.

- <u>Addictive behaviour</u> patterns or inordinate or <u>disproportionate affections</u>.
- <u>Overreacting emotionally</u> to stimulus that is not comparable to the response.
- Self-loathing, self-condemnation, self-dislike, negative self-talk, <u>insecurity</u>.
- Find it <u>difficult or uncomfortable to receive</u> compliments or receive praise.
- <u>Low self-esteem</u>, irrational fears or phobias, panic attacks, night terrors.
- Being <u>paranoid or hypochondriac</u>, fearful of harm or unexpected danger.
- Feelings of <u>depression</u>, rejection, failure, unforgiveness, regret, <u>lack of hope</u>.
- Pride or arrogance, unwillingness to listen to others, lying, <u>sinful cycles</u>.
- Jealousy, control issues, idolatry, bitterness, <u>unforgiveness</u>, religiosity.

- <u>Outbursts</u> of <u>anger and wrath</u> and <u>intense irrational hatred</u> for anyone.

Altars and Trading Platforms

An altar is a type of portal technology, what does that mean? It opens spiritual access points which allow transfer from one realm to another realm through dimensional gates (***1 Kings 18:38***).
It is a dimensional gateway system.

This is important to understand because an altar is built upon the pattern of the heart (***Psalm 51:16-17***), the heart is the most powerful dimensional gate in the universe (more on this in the 10 Revelations of the Glory of God Series, 'The Revelation of the Blood').

Since the beginning of time there have been Holy Altars consecrated to God which open the heavens into the kingdom realm from the earth realm (**Leviticus 9:24**). As stated before, this is a parallel to the heart an imitation that is designed to replicate the function of the spiritual heart (**Ecclesiastes 3:11**).

Sacrifices were offered upon such altars and prayers and petitions made towards them. Heavenly activity was present around altars and released upon their activation
(**1 Chronicles 21:26**).
Altars are activated by trading, a trade was made upon the altar, one thing for another thing
(**2 Chronicles 7**).

Should the trade be acceptable according to the correct protocols (which includes the authenticity of the pattern of the altar itself **Exodus 20:25**) power was transferred through the spiritual dimensional bridge, which was opened up in the unseen, at times physical fire manifested to consume the offering and exchange power systems between worlds (***Judges 6:21***).

So, what does this have to do with pulling down strongholds?
The demonic realm use altars also
(***Judges 6:25-26***).

Profane altars, evil altars, where dark transactions are made such as: curses, hexes, exchanges for power, influence, manipulation using dark powers to gain an upper hand illegally. It is a practice by those in the occult, pagan, satanists and new age. There is a reason the word 'altar' appears 364 times in the Bible and why God always instructed His people to destroy altars to other entities or gods, those altars are dimensional bridges to demonic activity and are conduits of massive amounts of spiritual chaos into an environment (tares among wheat situationally).

Deuteronomy 12:3 *And ye shall overthrow their altars, and break their pillars, and burn their groves with fire; and ye shall hew down the graven images of their gods and destroy the names of them out of that place.*

Evil altars require addressing with the word of God used like a weapon of obliteration to speak destruction and the throwing down of these altars.

For some people, their experience of repeated patterns of evil occurring in their lives could be the result of such operations.

Afterall an altar is not an entity, it is a technology, a mechanism... and a technology can be taken apart, and a mechanism can be damaged, jammed, caused to malfunction, or broken…

Exodus 20:25 *And if thou wilt make me an altar of stone, thou shalt not build it of hewn stone: for if thou lift up thy tool upon it, thou hast polluted it.*

Evil altars require destruction, otherwise it will continue communicating its programming into the spiritual atmosphere, as long as the altar is active, the demonic gate is active also.

Leviticus 26:30 *I then will destroy your high places, and cut down your incense altars, and heap your remains on the remains of your idols, for My soul shall abhor you.*

Numbers 33:52 *then you shall drive out all the inhabitants of the land from before you, and destroy all their figured stones, and destroy all* *their molten images and demolish all their high places;*

Deuteronomy 12:2 *You shall utterly destroy all the places where the nations whom you shall dispossess serve their gods, on the high mountains and on the hills and under every green tree.*

2 Kings 18:4 *He removed the high places and broke down the sacred pillars and cut down the Asherah. He also broke in pieces the bronze serpent that Moses had made, for until those days the sons of Israel burned incense to it; and it was called Nehushtan.*

2 Chronicles 31:1 *Now when all this was finished, all Israel who were present went out to the cities of Judah, broke the pillars in pieces, cut down the Asherim and pulled down the high places and the altars throughout all Judah and Benjamin, as well* *as in Ephraim and Manasseh, until they had destroyed them all. Then all the sons of Israel returned to their cities, each to his possession.*

2 Kings 17:11 *and there they burned incense on all the high places as the nations did which the Lord had carried away to exile before them; and they did evil things provoking the Lord.*

How can evil altars be detected?
If someone is experiencing reoccurring issues in their life and this individual has **no strongholds in them which is connected to that reoccurring issue** (which is rare) then this cycle of negative manifestations against their life, health, finances, relationships, business, ministry, family, wellbeing etc, may be due to altars of evil being used against them, to conjure or open dark doorways to demonic activity to infiltrate these areas of their lives. This is very prevalent in places heavily

affected by occultic practices such as witches and warlocks and other more direct satanic practices which in almost all cases involve blood rituals from a human source or an animal source of some kind, as well as cursing objects and giving them out under the false pretence of protection (dream catchers, evil eye pendants, idol statues etc).

Furthermore, items traded upon dark altars can be cursed, which means to be imbued or marked with negative energies or frequencies that can be sources of transmitting corruption from the altar that it has been tethered to. Like how a rope can connect two things together, that object will be connected to that dark altar by these energies until the connection is severed or the physical item itself destroyed, such items are mediums.

Deuteronomy 7:26 *Neither shalt thou bring an abomination into thine house, lest thou be*

*a cursed thing like it: but thou shalt utterly detest it, and thou shalt utterly abhor it; for it is
a cursed thing.*

The same on the positive can be for items that have been blessed, food, objects, cloth, oil, water. These can be mediums of transmitting divine energies through imbuing items with virtue.

Ezra 8:28 *And I said unto them, Ye are holy unto the Lord; the vessels are holy also; and the silver and the gold are a freewill offering unto
the Lord God of your fathers.*

Exodus 30:25 *And thou shalt make it
an oil of holy ointment, an ointment compound after the art of the apothecary: it shall be
an holy anointing oil.*

Acts 19:12 *So that from his body were brought unto the sick handkerchiefs or aprons, and the diseases* *departed from them, and the evil spirits went out of them.*

Altars are quite literally a demonic device to which the church, largely speaking, is quite ignorant of, especially in the western world we are to realise the warfare is very real and the enemy is an expert manipulator.

The devil is not able to create anything at all, but is a thief, so will steal, knowledge information and operations and patterns, is liar so will use deception and warped knowledge, a murderer so will always attempt to kill and destroy those whom God loves.

2 Corinthians 2:11 *Lest Satan should get an advantage of us: for we are not ignorant of his <u>devices.</u>*

Ephesians 6:11 *Put on the full armour of God, so*

*that you can make stand against the devil's schemes. **12**For our struggle is not against flesh and blood, but against the rulers, against the authorities, against <u>the powers of this world's darkness</u>, and against the <u>spiritual forces of evil</u> in the heavenly realms.*

The last point to note concerning altars is that because it is patterned after the heart of man (which is a similitude of the heart of God), an individual can also become an altar.

Someone who has a life of consecration to God to such a degree that they become an open gateway of heavenly transaction, then as the temple of the Lord, their heart has become activated as an exceedingly high functioning altar for God's purposes in bringing heaven to earth and their prayers are answered with power!

Their words carry spiritual weight, their inner life of obedience is counted as more valuable than a holy sacrifice and all the transactions of the heart are burning with a fire that never goes out within.

Romans 12:1 *I beseech you therefore, brethren, by the mercies of God, that ye present your bodies a living sacrifice, holy, acceptable unto God, which is your reasonable service.*

Mark 12:30 *And thou shalt love the Lord thy God with all thy heart, and with all thy soul, and with all thy mind, and with all thy strength: this is the first commandment.*

Colossians 3:23 *And whatsoever ye do, do it heartily, as to the Lord, and not unto men;*

Deuteronomy 30:6 *And the Lord your God will circumcise your heart and the heart of your* offspring, so that you will love the Lord your God with all your heart and with all your soul, that you may live.

Proverbs 27:19 *As in water face reflects face, so the heart of man reflects the man.*

Jeremiah 31:33 *But this is the covenant that I will make with the house of Israel after those days, declares the Lord: I will put my law within them, and I will write it on their hearts. And I will be their God, and they shall be my people.*

Psalm 40:8 *I delight to do your will, O my God; your law is within my heart."*

Jeremiah 29:13 *You will seek me and find me, when you seek me with all your heart.*

Psalm 19:14 *Let the words of my mouth, and the*

meditation of my heart, be acceptable in thy sight, O LORD, my strength, and my redeemer.

<u>Evil altars can be used to create the environmental factors to which strongholds are forged within</u>. Therefore, we need to target and destroy them and walk free from the chaos they release. As we throw down every evil device, altar and operation may we build the altar of the Lord in its place, and may we become living flames of fire as the living altar of our hearts burn for Jesus alone. Halleluiah!

For practical insight into targeting these devices in prayer that may be working against you please see the pulling down strongholds prayer from page <u>38</u>.

Pulling Down Strongholds Kit – Matthew Tucker

POSITIVELY CHARGED	NEUTRALLY CHARGED	NEGATIVELY CHARGED
Willing	Can have laws	Not subject to law of God
Set on things above	Can be the same as someone else's	Backwards & fixed
Mind of Christ		Vanity
Has wisdom		Lowly
Guarded by peace	Can have thoughts cast into it from within and without	Hardened
Forwards & growing		Wrong
Faithful		Doubtful
Right & correct	Can be set	Evil
Reliable		Reprobate
Ready	Can desire	Mind the flesh
Built up	Can have things called to it	Faint
Renewed		Double
Strong	Has a voice	Blinded
Mind the spirit	Can be full (mindful)	Corrupted
Flexible to God	Can have things on it	Bitter
Good		Grief
Virtuous	Can be inclined	Bad
Steadfast	Can be one	wicked
Full of thoughts that are: true, honest, just, pure, lovely, & of good report	Can be stayed on a thing	Despiteful
	Can have things come to it	Alienated
Loves God fully	Can have things enter it	
Subject to law of God	Can remember	
Sober/sound		

Strongholds when set in place, cause the mind to agree with thought patterns on the negatively charged spectrum of mind. The fortress of the Lord built in the mind, causes the positively charged spectrum of mind to be built up and established. If any of the above bullet points apply (pages 18, 19, 20, 37) in any case, then a stronghold is likely to be present and would need to be dealt with immediately and thoroughly.

A positively charged mind will not develop strongholds, even when under attack, it will hold its ground. Although such a mind may discern the attack, it will not be moved by it. A positively charged mind is built up and fortified by the fortress of the Lord and will not take onboard any bondages when in trial or under pressure.
 A negatively charged mind is predisposed towards having strongholds because it is already in a weakened state because of its own internal stress. It will believe the lies and fall under oppression.

However, the engrafted word of God is able to save the soul from being influenced by demonic attack, lies, influence or manipulation.

The word of God protects the soul and guards the mind with peace.

This is THE answer, "it is written…"

When Jesus was under attack from the enemy in the wilderness, He responded directly to the lies, trickery, and assault upon His mind. He won! Responding to the initial attacks always strips them of their power to slip through into the deeper recess of the mind undetected, the aim is to catch them while they are in mid motion, not once they have hit a certain target, intercept those thoughts first, then the eventuality of strongholds being built is reduced to zero percent.

Prevention is always better than a cure.

A – Z List of strongholds (if suffered from and gripped with, or doing)

Abuse; Abandonment; Addiction; Adultery; Anger; Arrogance; Bitterness; Condemnation; Control; Deception; Denial; Despair; Dishonesty; Disorganisation; Doubt; Drunkenness; Emulations (rivalry against someone); Envy; Fear; Fornication; Greed (food & material things); Grief; Hatred; Heresy; Idolatry; Ignorance; Irritation; Jealously; Judgmentalism; Lack of (anything you should have but don't e.g. focus, concentration, memory, etc); Lasciviousness; Laziness; Lying; Manipulation; Masturbation; Offence; People pleasing; Pornography; Poverty; Pride; Procrastination; Rejection; Revelry (out of control behaviour due to seeking fulfilment); Sedition (disrespect and contending against authority figures); Selfishness; Self-pity; Shame; Sorrow; Strife (striving for superiority over others); Torment; Uncleanness; Unforgiveness; Variance (contentious disagreeability); Vulnerability; Witchcraft.

How do we pull down strongholds?

Take a few minutes to be mindful of what categories may apply to your situation from the bullet points above and be ready to address it. Then find the scriptures in the word of God that speak of the direct opposite.

Let us go through this step by step.

It begins with submitting to God and then afterwards resisting the enemy.

ATMOSPHERE

I recommend putting on some instrumental worship music (soaking in his presence is good) and taking a few minutes to thank God in advance for the freedom that you are about to receive. Focus yourself on the presence of God.

DICERNMENT

Lord as you search my mind by Your Spirit, reveal to me every and any stronghold and structure within my mind that is not established by You.

THANKSGIVING
Give thanks to the Lord for his power and love, for His purposes for your life.

PRAISE
Give praise to Jesus for what he did on the cross to set you free from sin.

WORSHIP
Give him honour and worship to Him because He is worthy, and He is good.

REPENTANCE (forgive anyone you need to forgive, do so now)
Lord I repent for allowing the stronghold of _____ and for coming into agreement with this stronghold, and its effects over me I turn away from the stronghold of _____ and I ask for forgiveness now, and I receive Your forgiveness in this moment for participating with the building of this stronghold. I am accepted, washed, and loved by You Father… so I accept myself as one who is worth Your love, so I am worth my own love also, I will agree with Your love not disagree with it, I will

agree with Your choice to love me and receive Your love and allow my identity to be shaped by Your love for me.

I renounce all agreement with _____ I break all covenants with any evil spirit behind _____ and rebuke them by commanding them to get away from me, I curse all trading against my soul and command those trading platforms to BREAK NOW!

I bind every unclean spirit that is connected to every negative mindset which was formed in alignment with _____ and I dismantle them and their pathways of connection to me right NOW in Jesus' name by the power of the Holy Spirit and the weapons of God's warfare.

I repent of every incorrect belief system that has fed into the building of this stronghold and I ask the Holy Spirit as my Helper, to assist me in totally reversing it from this day forward. I receive every good thing in heavenly places in Christ for me.

I command every single evil altar that has supplied darkness into the atmosphere around my life to be destroyed now! Be consumed by judgement fire right now! I cancel every dark trade made against me and nullify the devices of the enemy, they malfunction immediately and cannot operate against me. NO WEAPON FORMED AGAINST ME SHALL PROSPER IN THE MIGHTY NAME OF JESUS!

Every high thing that has opposed the truth of the word of God comes down right NOW, from today I partner with the Lord and the angels to establish the fortress of the Lord in its place. By His precious promises I partake of His life and the divine nature.

The Kingdom of God within me is established in my spirit and anchored in my heart right now, which is **RIGHTEOUSNESS**, **PEACE,** and **JOY** in the Holy Spirit. I am righteous, I have peace, I live in Joy!

WARFARE (speak with force and power)
I utterly destroy the stronghold of _____ by the power of the Spirit and the truth of the word of God and I release the opposite right now in the

name of Jesus (declare the opposite **USE THE FRUIT OF THE SPIRIT** pick the fruit you need, see list **page 43**) I release peace over my heart and mind, I release the love of God over my soul. My mind is (Speak the **POSITIVELY CHARGED** mind **page 34**)

I drain every power supply used to build the stronghold of _____ and I pull it down now by the power of the word of God. I reject all manipulation and unclean spirits that have been working against me and I command them, GO RIGHT NOW in the mighty name of Jesus Christ. You have no more part in me.

I cast down every vain imagination that was used to supply energy into that stronghold and I replace it NOW: by the power of your imagination CHANGE any and all negative imaginations associated with the stronghold, for example: if it is fear of something bad happening, create the imagination of something good happening instead and thank God for it as you SEE the good; these are whatsoever things are true, honest, just, pure, lovely, and of good report.

See yourself in the good, acceptable, and perfect will of God and use the 5 senses as you do this.

I fully disassociate and disconnect myself from every evil stronghold and renounce all torment; it CANNOT abide here. I declare I am free. The Lord is my rock, my fortress, and my salvation my high tower and my place of refuge. I am saved!

I release over my soul the Spirit of glory, and I infuse the grace of the fruits of the spirit into my soul in every space where it is needed. I receive: **LOVE, JOY, PEACE, PATIENCE, GOODNESS, KINDNESS, GENTLENESS, FAITHFULNESS** and **SELF-CONTROL** which is from the **MIND OF CHRIST LOCATED WITHIN MY SPIRT.**

I AM a NEW CREATION, FULL of FREEDOM AND HARMONY, ALL THINGS IN ME ARE MADE NEW!

SPEAK (speak with strength, certainty, and care)
By the power of my spirit I speak to my brain right now and I govern it into life and freedom. I speak to my brain, and I command it to be corrected and to be reordered according to the patterns of LIFE and VICTORY. I speak new living connections to be formed NOW, BE created NOW! Positive structures be formed NOW, brain be healed in the name of Jesus, every disrepair BE REPAIRED NOW.

I speak to my body and the memory locked into my body and I release healing to my body right now, I receive healing, by His stripes I was healed, I speak healing to my memories locked within my body and I delete every record of trauma from my body and every left-over effect of any stronghold to permanently dissolve and be gone NOW.

PRAY & REJOICE
As you are led in any other way pray; pray in the Spirit (in tongues) worship God, release words of life into your future, commission angels to go ahead of you and around you. Command the

angels to remove every offensive thing from the atmosphere around your life, around your home, around your workplace.
Begin to intercede for blessing and breakthrough for yourself, your family, your work, your church, ministry, your neighbourhood, your nation, your leaders, government, pray for the body of Christ, the labourers in the harvest.

Declare His will be done His kingdom come on earth as it is in heaven. Amen. Rejoice! You are free. Now as a lifestyle, keep renewing your mind to truth, keep growing strong and fortifying yourself in your walk with the Lord. The stronghold is GONE, now partner with the Holy Spirit in building the fortress of the Lord and become totally unshakable. In Jesus' holy name amen.

END NOTE ON SOUL TIES
You can also use this to break soul ties by simply replacing the words <u>stronghold of</u> and the empty space with <u>soul ties with and filling in the empty space with the person's name</u> that you need to break soul ties with.

THREE DIMENSIONS OF FREEDOM

These three dimensions are fundamental to ensure one remains free and does not succumb to the wiles of the devil and his attempt to steal away the deliverance that we have received.

This book is support towards step one and two, but not step three, allow me to explain.

1. The first dimension required to ensure freedom is the **breaking of bondages**. Without the breaking of bondages which can include but is not limited to healing, deliverance, pulling down strongholds, throwing down dark altars, removal of cursed objects, or destroying their energy connections. Then it will be difficult to move onto the second stage and break through successfully, this is a higher level of freedom than the first.

Isaiah 10:27
Luke 10:19,

Mark 16:17-18,
James 5:14-15

2. The second dimension required to ensure freedom is the **renewing of the mind**. Unless one renovates the mental arena and elevates their thinking into superior realms of truth than they previously understood in a particular area, then freedom can be temporary and fleeting.

This can even go as far as a healing is concerned, not that someone can lose their healing per-se but they can still get sick again with the same, similar, or worse condition if their mind is not renewed concerning their identity and God's provision of healing, protection and heath for example.

Renewing the mind ensures that one is built up and edified in the truth so they can prove what the good, acceptable, and perfect will of God is, this is completely necessary to move beyond needing to experience victory, into actual experiential victory.

There are 2 ways to renew the mind, one of which is by loading the mental sphere with the correct information from the word of God rightly divided, believing, and then doing it, so one's heart and mind are aligned across the soul and then the right actions can be produced consistently.

The other way is by beholding Jesus and encountering Him and being changed into the same image from glory to glory by the glory. (For more information and systematic spirit filled tools on renewing the mind see 'Renewing the Mind 101' by Sophia Tucker).

Romans 12:1-2
2 Corinthians 3:18

3. The third dimension required to ensure freedom is **progressive conformity towards the patterns of freedom**. What this simply means is practically adjusting one's lifestyle and habits to eliminate the bondage factors and maximise the components that contribute towards a life of freedom. This is the go and sin no more lest a worse thing come upon you that Jesus was speaking of, to ensure due diligence to the freedom or forgiveness received.

A simple example for this is if one is delivered of an addiction and then renews their mind to their identity and value and their body as the temple of God, then the conformity would be getting rid of those substances, it would be not going to the places they used to go before to get them, or changing their previous company that was associated with their bondage. It may be changing their viewing habits, or the part of town they live in etc. However, the Lord leads to take practical steps to ensure they are experientially walking upon the narrow road that leads to life from this point forward.

To support a lifestyle of conformity to freedom would be things like… increased intimacy with God, abiding in God's presence, prayer, worship, reading and study of the word, regular fellowship, practically walking out the great commission, serving others etc. These three dimensions when combined ensure one will maintain their walk of victory and freedom in Christ and then take things to even higher places as they grow into Him in all things, free and rooted and grounded in Christ.

FRAMING AND REFRAMING

Hebrews 11:1 *Now faith is the substance of things hoped for, the evidence of things not seen.*

So, only faith exercised at the moment and released in the NOW carries actual substance, it carries the substance of hope itself.

Hebrews 11:3 *Through faith we understand that the worlds were framed by the word of God, so that things which are seen were not made of things which do appear.*

Faith was the framework in which the word of God built the worlds, the hope within God was made substance and held in place by God's own faith and trust in His own word. Faith is a bit like a picture frame that holds the picture of your hope in place, without faith the picture hasn't got a fixed position to be held in place and kept, faith keeps the substance of hope in the word of God active and moving in your life.

2 Corinthians 4:18 *While we look not at the things which are seen, but at the things which are not seen: for the things which are seen are temporal; but the things which are not seen are eternal.*

In this activity, we will be looking past the seen things and into the unseen things, into the eternal possibility of hope using the word of God as our anchor and using the faith He has given to us to frame up our hope in Him through His word.

Psalm 119:105 *Thy word is a lamp unto my feet, and a light unto my path.*

Ephesians 1:18 *The eyes of your understanding being enlightened; that ye may know what is the hope of his calling, and what the riches of the glory* *of his inheritance in the saints,*

Using the eyes of the heart, we will look into the light of God's word and know a different experience of events that we have experienced that may not have gone the way it should have, or could have, we will rewrite this record in our minds so that it matches the hope of His calling and the riches of His glorious inheritance in us.

Let's begin...

Isaiah 30:15 *For thus saith the Lord God, the Holy One of Israel; In returning and rest shall ye be saved; in quietness and in confidence shall be your strength: ...*

Psalm 46:10 *Be still, and know that I am God: ...*

In a state of quiet reflection, (perhaps include some light instrumental worship or soaking music) close your eyes, breathe slowly, and relax your mind and calm your body.

Quietly surrender yourself to God afresh, commit the eyes of your heart to Him, and commit your imagination, memory, will, desire, intellect, emotions, and all your senses to the Lord.

Rest for a moment and be still and know that He is God, know that He is with you as you are open to receive and be led by the Holy Spirit.

Thank the Holy Spirit for leading and guiding you in this process as you get ready to reframe the realities that you have previously experienced which have been recorded within you.

Ask the Holy Spirit to bring to remembrance a situation that He wants to reframe.

Now in your imagination, you can go back to this event or an event that was either traumatic or problematic, as led by the Lord, and rewind it back to the beginning before things went wrong and then press play, but this time replay the event in light of what the word of God says, reframe it from the negative to the positive.

For example, it may be a recent argument you had, instead of playing back the argument see the discussion being done correctly and an agreement being made, reconciliation and love and mutual respect and honour in peace, allow yourself to feel the joy and satisfaction, comfort and the presence of the Lord guiding you.
See yourself and the other confessing faults and forgiving and being healed of the hurts and pains, see the other person in light of the mercy and grace of God and see yourself likewise, now begin to thank God for the new framework, the new nope.

<u>Pause</u> be still and observe, ask the Holy Spirit if there is anything else He wants to show you, say to you or reveal to you in this.

Receive what the Lord is revealing to you and thank Him for this before you continue.
Be sure to document this vision in writing or audio so that you may run with it (**Hab 2:1-3**).
You can then carry this forward into the next situation that begins to play out in a similar way and you can now decide to draw on this new record

of information and revert to the positive playbook instead of the negative and redirect the problems that would usually arise towards the positive result with the word of God and the leading of the Spirit.

Perhaps you made a mistake in some way, go back and reframe it, but this time do it correctly.

This works with the future also, if you are worried or anxious about negative eventualities, frame it intentionally, project forward and see things playing out positively, use the word of God as you do this, and you can speak the scriptures out loud as you do so, allow yourself to feel the emotions of things going well, engage your senses and hold onto this future record of the good and bring it into your NOW faith so the substance of it is retained.
You will now discover that your previous fears and anxieties are gone.

Make covenants and agreements with God for the future and speak this out with your mouth. Identify any part of yourself that is involved in the framing process and include it in the agreement with the

Lord. For example… by the grace of God that empowers my heart with faith, I make covenant with you Lord God to respond in peace when my… <u>wife/ husband/ child/ friend/ colleague/ manager</u> says/does… <u>you always do/ why did you/ I can't believe that/ you are just</u>… and I know You will help me Holy Spirit, I expect You to help me and I am in readiness of Your help towards me in this, I include my… <u>mind/ emotions/ intellect/ reasoning/ memories/ imagination/ eyes/ ears/ hands/ feet/ heart/ mouth</u> in this covenant with You Holy Father and I yield it to You for refining, I set my expectation on good only and not bad, I will allow You to direct my way before during and after this situation.

Job 31:1 I made a covenant with mine eyes; why then should I think upon a maid?

This is a very powerful tool, so practice using this in your quiet time with the Lord. You can over time, partner with the Holy Spirit and literally delete old negative bits of information from your mind and soul and overwrite them with positives, you may still in some cases remember the negative situation, however, you will find the sting of it is no more, the edge is taken away, the pain of it removed.

'Framing' is really useful for futureproofing against potential strongholds being formed in the first place, and **'Reframing'** is brilliant at interrupting the cycle of a potential stronghold in mid development and deconstructing it before it can solidify.

An additional tool to use in conjunction with Framing is moving through the framing process and establishing the fortress of the Lord. This is reverse engineering the process of building strongholds and establishing the fortress of the Lord, this is a useful flow process in mind renewal that you can use and put into practice.

BUILDING THE FORTRESS OF THE LORD - IN YOUR MIND

Add to your faith... renewing the mind milestone points...

THE SCRIPTUAL CONTEXT

2 Peter 1:5-10 KJVS
And beside this, giving all diligence, add to your

faith (pistis-restful confidence in God according to the knowledge of His will and word to hook into the realities of God) virtue; and to

virtue (arete-courage and moral uprightness and honesty) knowledge; **[6]** And to

knowledge (gnosis-intelligence and understanding, reason and considered thought) temperance; and to

temperance (egkrateia-self-control and mastery over your emotions) patience; and to

patience (hupomonē-hopeful endurance, patience and consistency, reliable steadfastness) godliness; **[7]** And to

godliness (eusebeia-holiness and reverence towards God, being mindful of God at all times in all things) brotherly kindness; and to

brotherly kindness (philadelphia-loving kindness and a sensitive cherishing of the people of God and your family)

charity (agapē-benevolence, the God kind of love).

[8] For if these things be in you, and abound, <u>they make you that ye shall neither be barren nor unfruitful in the knowledge of our Lord Jesus Christ.</u> **[9]** But he that lacketh these things is blind, and cannot see afar off, and hath forgotten that he was purged from his old sins. **[10]** Wherefore the rather, brethren, give diligence to make your calling and election sure: <u>for if ye do these things, ye shall never fall</u>:

2 Peter 1:11-13 KJVS
For so an entrance shall be ministered unto you abundantly into the everlasting kingdom of our Lord and Saviour Jesus Christ. **[12]** *Wherefore I will not be negligent to* **put you always in remembrance** *of these things,* **though ye know them**, *and* **be established in the present truth**. **[13]** *Yea, I think it meet, as long as I am in this tabernacle, to* **stir you up by putting you in remembrance**;

Philippians 4:8 KJVS
Finally, brethren, whatsoever things are **<u>true</u>**, *whatsoever things are* **<u>honest</u>**, *whatsoever things are* **<u>just</u>**, *whatsoever things are* **<u>pure</u>**, *whatsoever things are* **<u>lovely</u>**, *whatsoever things are of* **<u>good report</u>**; *if there be any* **<u>virtue</u>**, *and if there be any* **<u>praise</u>**, **think** *on these things.*

Colossians 3:2 KJVS
Set your affection on things above, *not on things on the earth.*

Romans 12:2 *And be not conformed to this world: but* **be ye transformed by the renewing of your mind, that ye may prove what is that good, and acceptable, and perfect, will of God.**

Pulling Down Strongholds Kit – Matthew Tucker

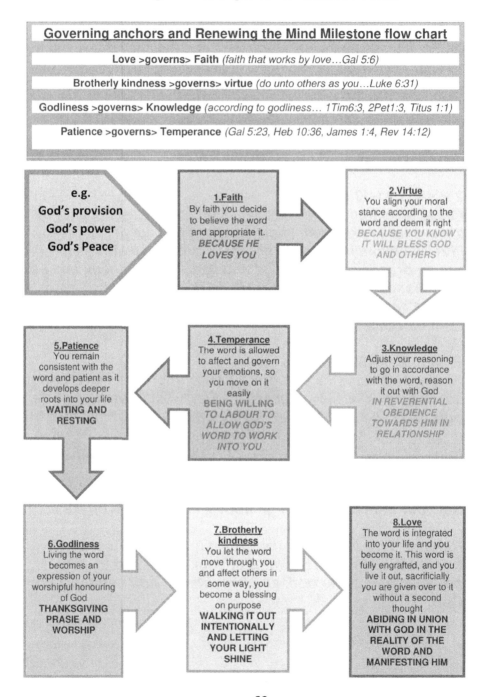

In the process of establishing the fortress of the Lord you can see what stage you are presently moving through… and what is required for the intentional level of partnership with God's word towards the integration and application of His word on a particular topic.

For example…

After pulling down the stronghold of unbelief in someone's life, they want to fill the place with the opposite and establish a fortress of the Lord in the precise place where the stronghold was.

Say it was unbelief in the power of God in working in the miraculous, perhaps they were of the cessation ideology or another denomination who have a form of godliness but deny the power (**2 Timothy 3:5**). After seeing from the scriptures that it is true and going through the process of pulling down strongholds, breaking altars and reframing, they want to establish the fortress of the Lord concerning the power of God and the working of miracles.

1.Then you could using the flowchart **gather scriptures** on the power of God and turn each of them into a **personal statement of faith** concerning the power of God and **set your trajectory**.
You can form a **decree statement** that states something like "I will experience the power of God in my life because it is God's will".

2. **Engage your conscience** and **dialogue with the Holy Spirit** about the **moral implications** of God's power at work in and through you, considering the **nature of God** and **His will**.

3. **Study** the power of God, **totally immerse** and be baptised in the knowledge of it, **engage your reasoning and intellect, take courses, watch videos, read accounts, read books** on it.

Search for **living examples today**, watch how they operate in the power of God and **fill your senses with it**, go to **conferences, talk about it**, get around those who **experience** and **live it**.

4. **Engage your emotions**, purposefully **set your desire on** encountering this **for yourself, pray it, ask, seek, knock,** and **receive**.

Praise God for giving it to you, **worship Him** for He IS it. Allow how you **feel** to become **enriched** by the **touch of God** in this area.

Rejoice with those who rejoice in it and **allow the conviction** and the **mourning of the Lord** in you for those who do not experience this and **feel how Jesus feels** about this, knowing how **He suffered and died to provide this grace** also through **the cross.**

5. This is a **marathon**, not a sprint, we must **engage patience and self-control**.

We **engage the will**, and our **memories** to call forth His word, to **stay the course** and **to not grow weary**, it may not manifest all at once, but **keep going, never quit, keep to the narrow way that leads to life, desire, be zealous, be passionate.**
Now, you can **wait on the Lord** having gone through **all the other stages** whilst **keeping on moving**

forward towards this reality being made manifest, you **are waiting ACTIVELY on the Lord.**
Waiting is **never passive**; you are engaged in **eager expectation and are hopeful.**

This is the stage where **deeper meditation** comes in, **engage your imagination, visualising, seeing yourself in it, walking it out, living it out, acting it out, role playing it out.**

In this stage you may start to have many **dreams** about it as **the Lord communicates back to you** on the establishing of this fortress in your mind. You may have **visions** of it, you may even start to receive **words from the Lord**, this **waiting state** is **powerful**.

It is here where the roots of the seed of His word **goes deep** very quickly.

6. This is where things start to go to **a new level**, this is where the **breakthrough** starts to **manifest**.
The godliness stage, where you now are **positioned within the fortress itself** and begin to **explore** it.

New angelic support is often assigned at this stage, as well as the angels that co-labour with you already are **now able to accomplish more**.

As you elevate in revealing the glory of God **the active participation of the angelic** is able increase also.

This is the appropriation of **the likeness of God** in this area, hence <u>godliness</u>, you **begin to start to operate <u>like God</u>** in this area and manifestation takes place, if it is in miracles as per this example then miracles start to manifest through you.

The expression of your faith explodes and **feeds into the beginning** of the process (from step 1) all over again and then the **cycle starts to overlap upon itself and expands**, beginning to **affect other areas of your life positively**, the **transferability** of this godliness stage now **causes ripples** throughout your whole being and walk of life in the Lord, spirit, soul and body. **People will begin to see** this aspect of **Christ growing and being formed in and through you**, coming alive.

7. Now, **living in the light of this fortress** becomes something that **starts to define fundamental** and **practical** elements of your life.

You **make room for it** now, you **look for opportunities** to **manifest this**, you would tend to take **further study** to **go deeper in honing** your abilities in manifesting and expressing this reality which has now become **a way of life**.

Some at this stage **find a mentor**, and/or **mentoring resources** (if they haven't done so already), either way, they are **being taught of the Lord** and the **7 Spirits of God are very active in their maturation process** in a big way.

It is in this stage, where some would often **begin ministry** in a higher capacity, and this **gift, calling, virtue, fruit, nature, characteristic** or **grace** will **become a foundational aspect** of their ministry and how they are **known to operate and function** by those in the body of Christ and the world even as you **let your light SO shine purposefully**.

Now you become **committed to your life being a permanent revelation of who God is** through you in this.

8. Final stage, **love**, **charity**.
As He is so are we in this world.

God is love.

So, **we too become love**.

We become so **one with this aspect of God** that it is indistinguishable where God starts, and we end in this area.

There is a **blurring of the lines of flow**, a **mysterious obscurity of the boundaries** where **heavenly things flow to the earth through us** and we are an **open gateway of God** in this area and **He flows through us**, unhindered, unrestrained.

We **are** this way now, **simply** as an **instrument of His love**, **we simply are**.

His love is our driving force now more than ever, we find **great intimacy and sensitivity,** and our walk with God starts to increase, as now we **know Him more deeply** though this.

We are in **conscious and functional union** with God in this area, the fortress of the Lord in our life is **adorned** and **radiant** inside and out, **radiating light** and shining through our **thoughts**, **words,** and **deeds**.

Our body is a living sacrifice to this, **our bodies yield their members joyfully in adoration**.

We **BECOME** the **worship itself.**
Our life BECOMES the praise.

Our very **breath** is His **love.**
This is the result of the **renewed mind.**

_____

Allow the presence of the Lord to embrace you as you grow.

You are not alone, remember the unseen is more real than the seen and you can cause the unseen faith realities to be more real to you than the natural seen realities.

Praise God.

Let His word become MORE real to you from now on. May this book bless you. Amen.

For more information or assistance in any of these topics, or if you need healing, deliverance, baptism in water or in the Holy Spirit, feel free to get in contact and I will be happy to help. God bless you.
ekballoministries@gmail.com

Printed in Great Britain
by Amazon